R

ALAN SUTTON PUBLISHING LIMITED

Alan Sutton Publishing Limited
Phoenix Mill · Far Thrupp · Stroud
Gloucestershire · GL5 2BU

First published 1995

Cover photographs: (front) a rear turret view of the 1953 Battle of Britain Day formation; (back) the Shackleton MR.3 of 220 Squadron suffers a nose wheel collapse, 1957.

British Library Cataloguing in Publication Data.
A catalogue record for this book is available from the British Library.

ISBN 0–7509–1030–5

Typeset in 9/10 Sabon.
Typesetting and origination by
Alan Sutton Publishing Limited.
Printed in Great Britain by
Ebenezer Baylis, Worcester.

For Ben

Nimrod – the Mighty Hunter.

Contents

ROYAL AIR FORCE STATION
ST. MAWGAN
VIGILA

Introduction

Royal Air Force St Mawgan has a proud history of maritime flying that spans over half a century of aeronautical activity. It sits nearly 400 ft above sea-level, overlooking the Atlantic Ocean. Early recorded flying activities from the site include mention in the pre-war *AA Register of Aircraft Landing Grounds* published by the Automobile Association to assist private pilots.

On 27 August 1933 Alan Cobham's National Aviation Display operated from the 40 acre site known as Trebelzue Big Field. Six years later the Weston-super-Mare based airline, Western Airways, opened a Manchester–Penzance service, calling at Barnstaple (North Devon) airport. On the same day, a twice-daily Swansea–Barnstaple–Newquay (Trebelzue)–Penzance (St Just) service, operated with DH84 Dragons, was also inaugurated by Western Airways. The Dragon, a twin-engined biplane, carried six passengers in addition to the pilot, usually John Dade, an experienced and skilful flyer who had previously been employed as a flying instructor with an associated company at Ramsgate Airport.

However, war clouds were darkening the Cornish skies and the outbreak of war saw all civilian flying banned and the Trebelzue site requisitioned as a satellite for nearby RAF St Eval. Two hard-surfaced runways were constructed, enabling minimal flying activities to take place from December 1941. On 30 December the requirement for aircraft to serve in the Middle East saw 44 Group of Ferry Command establish operations at Trebelzue, with personnel of No 2 Overseas Aircraft Despatch Unit (2 OADU) at nearby RAF Portreath transferring to the new station.

Using Gibraltar as a staging post, deliveries of aircraft from Trebelzue to the Middle East were commenced, although a combination of short runways and frequent crosswinds meant that RAF Trebelzue did not measure up to its designated role.

At the end of April 1942, discussions centred on the possible development of the site, to enable 44 Group to ferry one hundred aircraft per month to the Middle East. The solution was to construct a new airfield to the east of Trebelzue. The old airfield would then serve as a dispersal area for the new station, which would boast three runways. In the meantime, the activities of the gunnery school at Penhale Camp saw No. 1 Anti-Aircraft Co-operation Unit (1 AACU) operating its Hawker Henleys as target tugs over the Penhale range while flying from Trebelzue.

At this time the culinary fare offered by the officers' mess at Trebelzue was gaining considerable fame, resulting in royal patronage when, on 10 July, HRH The Duke of Kent visited the station, with his tour of inspection including a visit to the mess!

At the turn of the year, the Mustangs of 400 Royal Canadian Air Force (RCAF) Squadron, together with the Mosquitoes of 264 Squadron, were flying 'Instep' patrols over the south-west approaches in an attempt to counter the threat posed by German long-range fighters. However, the inadequacy of the airfield quickly resulted in 400 (RCAF) Squadron returning to its former base at Middle Wallop during January, while the Mosquitoes made the short hop to Portreath the following month.

Trebelzue was then left to the Henleys of 1602 and 1604 Flights. These had abandoned the water-logged grass airfield at Cleave, which in more recent years has become home to a Combined Signals Organization station.

On 24 February 1943 the airfield was renamed RAF St Mawgan. Although the occupants, a detachment of Henleys from 1 AACU at Cleave together with a small number of ferry movements, were a reminder of earlier activities at the base, the immediate future of St Mawgan lay in the hands of the United States Army Air Force (USAAF) which arrived in June in the shape of 491st Base & Air Base Squadron, Air Transport Command. The Americans then began a long wartime affinity with the station, with the first of the new runways being declared open on 1 July.

Fittingly, in view of the American tenancy, the first aircraft to use the new runway was a B–24 Liberator with a B–17 Flying Fortress as the second movement. The following month, with the remaining new runways opened, Trebelzue was relegated to a dispersal area. Meanwhile St Mawgan's enhanced facilities resulted in a considerable increase in aircraft movements with the USAAF dispatching large numbers of aircraft to North Africa during the late summer and early autumn. The station also quickly became established as the terminal for worldwide flights either arriving in or departing from the UK.

On 5 November, two USAAF Met Flights equipped with eight B–17s arrived at St Mawgan for a three month deployment. The airfield was quickly becoming overcrowded, as 2 OADU was continuing to dispatch aircraft from the station. However after little more than two weeks had elapsed, the Met Flights were posted.

Any lull in operations was filled by Dakotas operated by BOAC, which were tasked from 20 November with maintaining a United Kingdom–Algiers service of which the outbound route was Bristol (Whitchurch)–St Mawgan–Gibraltar–Algiers, and which returned via Rabat and Gibraltar. Aircraft had military markings and the crews wore RAF Reserve uniforms. The service terminated originally at Lisbon where the BOAC and Lufthansa check-in counters faced each other and shared the same baggage scales, despite the Dakotas being considered fair game by the Luftwaffe as they skirted the Bay of Biscay!

Activities at St Mawgan were not without incident as 1943 drew to a close. On 21 December four American servicemen died when a USAAF B–24 crashed near St Columb. The cliff-top runway left few options in the event of problems during take-off, which was illustrated graphically when a US Navy PB4Y–1 patrol bomber leaving St Mawgan for a transatlantic flight went over the cliff top and crashed into the sea below. All thirteen Navy men lost their lives, while five USAAF personnel were drowned when they were cut off by the incoming tide and the rescue attempt thwarted. The PB4Y–1 crew members were all returning to the USA having completed a tour of operations that amounted to thirty sorties or three hundred hours' flying time.

The early months of 1944 were a period of consolidation at St Mawgan with highlights that included completion of the hardstandings, a new control tower and the extension of the main 32/14 runway. In addition, the remaining domestic accommodation at Trebelzue was vacated as space became available at the new station. Requisitioned hotels and dwelling houses in Newquay provided sick quarters for Women's Auxiliary Air Force (WAAF) personnel and transit accommodation. Some members of the 491st Base & Air Base Squadron were also billeted in the town.

On 1 March, the BOAC operation through St Mawgan was joined by Transport Command passenger services at a time when the airfield was becoming established, although the following months would not be without incident. Again the sea was to claim victims when a Warwick of 525 Squadron, outbound on the Port Natal/Algiers service, crashed on take-off with a loss of sixteen lives.

Later that year, on 4 September, and despite St Mawgan's enviable weather record, a Dakota of 28 Squadron, South African Air Force, arrived over the fog-bound airfield from Algiers. With no option but to land, the pilot put the Dakota down close to Delabole without loss of life although the aircraft was a write-off.

Two months later BOAC was able to transfer its St Mawgan stop to Hurn when the improving military situation permitted the opening of more direct routes across France. Meanwhile the Americans had installed an SBS51 Instrument Landing System (ILS) for the main runway. Training on the new facility was provided by the Airspeed Oxford-equipped 1529 Radio Aids Training Flight.

Meanwhile, the air war against Germany ground on relentlessly, the aircraft of Bomber Command attacking the heart of Germany by night while the B–17s and B–24s of the USAAF 8th Air Force flew daylight formation raids. Frequently the bombers would return to find their bases in eastern England fog-bound, with only a handful of airfields, including St Mawgan, still open.

Further formations featured at St Mawgan during the summer of 1945 when, with the cessation of hostilities in Europe, USAAF and RCAF squadrons started out on their homeward-bound transatlantic flights from St Mawgan. The station was now designated RAF Transport Command's No. 1 Diversion Centre, becoming the UK departure point for heavy aircraft reinforcements for the Far East. Similarly the new French Air Force received many aircraft that were ferried through St Mawgan en route to France.

On 9 July 1946, a complete squadron of sixteen Lancasters set out from their base at Graveley on a goodwill tour to the USA. The aircraft, Lancaster B.1s (FEs) of 36 Squadron, went via St Mawgan and the Azores to Mitchell Field, accompanied by an Avro York. The aircraft visited American aerodromes, including San Antonio, Kelly and Andrews Field, and participated in the Air Force Day celebrations at Long Beach, as a token of the war-winning alliance of the USAAF and RAF.

The first chapter of St Mawgan's history closed when, on 1 July 1947, the station was placed on Care & Maintenance, a situation that would prevail for the next four years.

During 1949, rumour was rife in Cornwall that St Mawgan was to be reopened as a base for United States Air Force (USAF) B–36 bombers in view of increasing tension between East and West. The rumour proved unfounded although the giant bombers of Strategic Air Command (SAC) became familiar sights at other UK bases, including Brize Norton and Fairford.

For the next two years the airfield lay quiet, although the summer of 1949 saw the Plymouth & District Aero Club offering pleasure flights to holidaymakers. The following summer saw a Manchester–Newquay service inaugurated by Finland Aviation. Although short lived, the service pointed to a future of regular services and the construction of a civil air terminal to serve as Newquay Airport.

However, it was not B–36s but Lancasters that would next operate from the station when, during April 1951, the initial elements of Coastal Command's School of Maritime Reconnaissance (SMR) arrived at St Mawgan, in preparation for the arrival of the unit's Lancaster MR.3 aircraft that were deployed to the airfield during June. Tasked as maritime reconnaissance trainers, the Lancasters had previously been converted to ASR.III standard including the fitment of ASV radar and the removal of the dorsal turret. Later modified to GR.3 standard, the aircraft were later re-designated as MR.3s.

Once again Newquay hotels doubled as station accommodation when winter weather highlighted the appalling condition of many of the old wartime

St Mawgan's last Shackleton.

buildings that would eventually be replaced as the refurbished station took shape. Officers had to borrow eating irons and mugs from airmen who benefited from the only functioning mess on the station. Clearly the task of the station commander, Gp. Capt. O.A. Morris DSO, was above and beyond the normal terms of reference of a station's master!

The Battle of Britain air display held during September 1952 drew an unexpected participant in the shape of a Convair RB–36H from the USAF's 72nd Bomb Wing. The strategic reconnaissance version of the six-engined B–36H bomber had suffered an engine failure resulting in an emergency landing and subsequent support from a C–47 that arrived in Cornwall carrying a spare engine.

During the station's 1953 Battle of Britain Air Display on 19 September, twelve SMR Lancasters made a spectacular sight. The aircraft were lined up facing the crowd and, on the command of the leader, each aircraft's engine was started up simultaneously – 3, 4, 2, 1 – and then the formation was taxied in line, in front of the crowd, and lined up for a mass take-off. A participant in the formation recollects that the last flight of four aircraft enjoyed a turbulent ride!

In the interim the SMR was joined at the station by the Air Sea Warfare Development Unit (ASWDU) and 744 Squadron of the Fleet Air Arm (FAA). The latter unit, commanded by Lt.-Cdr. F.G.J. Arnold RN and equipped with Firefly AS.6s, had earlier been re-formed at Culdrose as the Naval Air-Sea Warfare Development Unit, to work in conjunction with the ASWDU. Trials carried out under code names such as 'Talbe', 'Homer' and 'Random' were conducted with the Fireflies, which were joined and eventually replaced by Gannets, Avengers and Sea Furies. Trials during 1954 by the ASWDU also included experiments with a Shackleton fitted with a Magnetic Anomaly Detection (MAD) 'stinger' tail.

On 11 June 1955, 744 Squadron formed an 'X' Flight for radar jamming trials. The squadron was restyled the Naval Anti-Submarine Development Squadron in February 1956 and two months later undertook dummy rocket projectile dives over the Lilstock Range. The squadron disbanded on 31 October 1956 owing to the Suez situation.

Meanwhile, the summer of 1954 had seen the HQ establishment of 22 Squadron arrive from Thorney Island. The squadron's Search & Rescue (SAR) Whirlwinds were serviced at St Mawgan on behalf of the unit's detached flights, although a further two years would elapse before 'A' Flight, with a pair of operational Whirlwinds, would come on line at the Cornish station.

As the summer of 1956 drew to a close, another proud chapter of RAF history was about to end. The disbandment of the SMR at the end of September would result in the withdrawal from service of the RAF's last Lancaster aircraft. This was the bomber that had taken the war to Berlin and the very heartland of Germany, and had gained worldwide fame after 617 Squadron's devastating attack on the Ruhr dams. 'You are present at the end of an aircraft era,' said the station commander, Gp. Capt. D.R.S. Bevan-John at the station's 1956 Battle of Britain 'At Home' when the Lancasters were publicly displayed for the last time.

The following month, a formation of St Mawgan's Lancasters made a farewell flypast at each of Coastal Command's UK bases, culminating in a ceremony on 15 October, when Wg. Cdr. E.J. Brookes DFC lifted RF325 from the runway for the last time and set course for Wiltshire and the breakers at Wroughton.

The disbandment of the SMR and the transfer of the unit's task to the Maritime Operational Training Unit at Kinloss enabled the St Eval-based Shackleton squadrons, 220 and 228, to re-deploy to St Mawgan's longer runways. The move, made during December 1956, enabled 220 Squadron to receive the Shackleton MR.3, an improved Shackleton variant which incorporated a tricycle undercarriage, duplicated landing wheels, a modified mainplane with revised planform, improved ailerons, wingtip auxiliary tanks and a clear-vision flight deck canopy.

The summer of 1957 saw a pair of South African Air Force Shackleton MK.3s arrive at St Mawgan for crew training. Participation in a joint tactical exercise with Coastal Command over the North Sea followed, prior to the aircraft being ferried to South Africa and their new base at D.F. Malan Airport, where a total of eight Shackletons were eventually delivered to 35 Squadron.

During January 1958, 206 Squadron also relocated from St Eval as the second MR.3 squadron at St Mawgan. In October, 220 Squadron was renumbered 201 Squadron, while 42 Squadron also moved to the station, enabling neighbouring St Eval to be placed on Care & Maintenance, its runways being inadequate for maximum-weight operations by the Shackleton MR.3.

On 6 January 1958, the Whirlwind-equipped 1360 Flight formed at St Mawgan and remained established until 1 February, when it became 217 Squadron. It then moved to Christmas Island as part of a combined force supporting the nuclear tests being carried out there.

During the summer of 1959, Starways Ltd of Liverpool introduced a Liverpool–Newquay service with Dakotas and DC–4s. The service, whose route went via Exeter Airport, was operated on Saturdays and was aimed at holidaymakers who would otherwise have to negotiate the delays of the notorious Exeter bypass and a national road system mainly devoid of motorways and dual carriageways.

Although the Shackleton MR.3s settled down to largely unpublicized patrolling of the sea lanes, the records show that during February 1959, Flt. Lt. D.R. Foster and crew from 206 Squadron remained airborne for the record time of 24 hours 21 minutes during a patrol to the Canaries. The same year, a Shackleton MR.3 of 201 Squadron, equipped with special instrumentation, left St Mawgan on a round-the-world flight via India, Australia, New Zealand, Christmas Island, Hickam (Hawaii), North Island, Kelly and Norfolk (USA) and Greenland.

During the early summer of 1960, BOAC returned to St Mawgan, when the airline based its newly delivered Boeing 707 aircraft at the airfield, for crew training. The uncluttered Cornish airspace was considered ideal for the purpose.

A perceived change in the Soviet submarine threat saw 201 Squadron take up station at Kinloss during March 1965, to be joined four months later by 206 Squadron. In exchange, the Kinloss-based Maritime Operational Training Unit (MOTU), equipped with the Shackleton T.4, moved to St Mawgan. Modified internally to reproduce the radio and navigation fit of the MR.3, the T.4s were conversions from elderly Shackleton MR.1 and 1As.

Meanwhile 42 Squadron remained at St Mawgan and on 14 July 1966 received its standard from Her Majesty the Queen, who accepted an invitation to open the new officers' mess.

During August 1969 a decision that would have long-term effects on the security and policing of Northern Ireland was made at St Mawgan. Home Secretary James Callaghan, flying from London to Culdrose to meet Premier Harold Wilson, was diverted to St Mawgan when Culdrose became fog-bound. At St Mawgan he met the Prime Minister, who had been flown by helicopter from his holiday home in the Scillies. The two then discussed the deteriorating situation in Belfast and Londonderry, before making the momentous decision to send soldiers into Northern Ireland.

By now the days of the piston-engined Shackleton in the front-line maritime role with the RAF were numbered – the first production Nimrod MR.1 had flown on 28 June 1968. The first land-based four-jet maritime reconnaissance aircraft to enter service in any of the world's air forces, the Nimrod was equipped with state of the art anti-submarine technology. With an on-station patrol time of more than six hours and a range of 1,150 miles, the Nimrod coupled the ability to make a quick dash to the search area and a fast return to base, with an airfield performance that enabled it to operate from all the RAF's contemporary 'maritime' runways.

The first Nimrods joined the newly re-formed 236 Operational Conversion Unit (OCU) at St Mawgan during October 1969, tasked with converting Shackleton crews. The Nimrod joined 201 Squadron at Kinloss the following summer prior to 42 Squadron converting at St Mawgan in April 1971. Both the OCU and 42 Squadron operated their aircraft in a pool, with the station operating a centralized servicing system in the purpose-built hangar that now dominated the Cornish landscape.

During May 1970, 7 Squadron re-formed at St Mawgan in the target facilities role, equipped with a variety of marks of Canberra including the TT.18. Tasked with presenting targets at heights and speeds which simulated a potential enemy aircraft, in order to test missile and gun positions at locations around the British Isles, the squadron hauled a variety of targets from the simple drogue to the complex Rushton long-tow target system. Developed by Flight Refuelling Ltd, the Rushton system replaced earlier drone targets which were becoming prohibitively expensive with the increased accuracy of surface-to-air weaponry.

The system comprised a pair of underwing winches capable of holding 48,200 ft of cable, a launcher (which both released and recovered the target in flight) and the target itself, an 8ft finned cylinder. The winch, which was fully automatic, controlled the reeling out of the target by means of a ram air turbine (a three-bladed propeller), which also supplied the power for recovery.

Up from St Mawgan, a Canberra TT.18 of 7 Squadron.

The squadron also provided 'silent targeting' facilities for Army and Navy exercises, providing the aircraft as low and fast targets for radar and unloaded guns to track. The squadron, which had originally taken on much of the work of the Exeter-based 3 Civilian Anti-Aircraft Co-operation Unit (3 CAACU), disbanded at St Mawgan at the end of 1982.

A further departure was 236 OCU, now with dual identity as 37 (Reserve) Squadron, which transferred base to Kinloss. Meanwhile 42 Squadron, as the sole surviving St Mawgan-based Nimrod unit, remained in Cornwall until 1992, when it too joined the Kinloss Maritime Reconnaissance Wing, taking up 236 OCU's role as 42 (Reserve) Squadron, with responsibility for the conversion training of Nimrod aircrew.

During the spring of 1994, the Ministry of Defence (MoD) announced that a new £13 million Joint Maritime Communications Centre would become operational at St Mawgan during April 1995. Commanded by Capt. Pamela Mulvehill of the US Navy (USN), the facility provides a secure communications centre for fleet support for the USN in the Atlantic, the centre would also serve both the Royal Navy and RAF Strike Command. Financed jointly by the UK MoD and the US, the £100 million operations centre comprises a buried and hardened communications building approximately 70 metres square within the perimeter of St Mawgan. The £2.2 million refurbishment of barracks would include a new dental and medical centre together with education, fitness and religious facilities. Other plans included an 18,000 sq ft retail centre to serve the 200-plus US servicemen and their families expected to be employed at the base from 1998.

Bringing the St Mawgan story up to date, nearby RAF Portreath, the home of 405 Signals Unit, ceased to be an independent unit during May 1995, when it became a satellite station of St Mawgan as part of the 'Options for Change' defence review. During the run-down ceremony, three flights of station personnel marched past the reviewing officer, Air Cmdr. Cliff Spinks, Senior Air Staff Officer, No. 11 Group. The outgoing station commander, Sqn. Ldr. Nick Warrick, handed over the keys to Gp. Capt. Mike Trace, station commander of St Mawgan.

Portreath will be run down from its current strength of 150 personnel to around 80, but will continue its task of providing radar coverage over the south-western approaches of the UK.

Currently St Mawgan is home to HQ 22 Squadron, the Sea King Training Unit; No. 2625 (County of Cornwall) Field Squadron, Royal Auxiliary Air Force (RAuxAF) Regiment; The School of Combat Survival & Rescue; No. 3 Maritime Headquarters (County of Devon) (RAuxAF); and the Search & Rescue Helicopter Engineering Squadron.

As a cornerstone of the Cornish economy the airfield, with a newly extended civil air terminal, continues to double as Newquay Airport. During the autumn of 1995 the first inclusive tour holiday flight from Newquay was established. A 150-seater Boeing 737 flight to Malta called at the Cornish airport to collect holidaymakers while en route from Exeter to Malta. In addition Brymon Airways continues to operate its scheduled London–Newquay service, in British Airways colours, with a fleet of five modern De Havilland Dash 7 quiet STOL airliners.

Keith A. Saunders, 1995

Personnel from various trades at St Mawgan pictured in front of a DH Mosquito, probably during August 1945. Len Brown, on the extreme left of the back row, was serving in the Royal Navy but was attached to the station as an electrician.

COMMANDING OFFICERS	DATE OF APPOINTMENT
Sqn. Ldr. R. Barry-Martin MC	30 December 1941
Wg. Cdr. G. Burges DFC	3 March 1942
Wg. Cdr. Sir R.H. Barlow AFC	13 June 1943
Gp. Capt. R.P.P. Pope DFC, AFC	27 June 1943
Gp. Capt. J.C.A. Johnson	8 August 1944
Gp. Capt. W.E. Purdin	6 October 1944
Gp. Capt. T.B. Bruce MC	8 December 1944
Gp. Capt. A.M. Rodgers	1 July 1946
Station closed	January 1947–March 1951
Gp. Capt. O.A. Morris DSO	16 April 1951
Gp. Capt. G.G. Barrett CBE	15 October 1951
Gp. Capt. G.S.A. Parnaby OBE	11 August 1953
Gp. Capt. J.M.N. Pike DSO, DFC	18 July 1955
Gp. Capt. D.R.S. Bevan-John OBE	1 March 1956
Gp. Capt. W.D. Hodgkinson DFC, AFC, ADC	5 January 1959
Gp. Capt. E.F.J. O'Doire DFC, AFC	15 February 1961
Gp. Capt. D.S. Lindsay OBE, AFC	1 May 1963
Gp. Capt. J.R. Saunders	11 June 1965
Gp. Capt. K.J. Barratt	8 December 1967
Gp. Capt. P.M. Harvey	26 May 1970
Gp. Capt. D.A. Arnott DFC, AFC	9 June 1972
Gp. Capt. H.M. Archer AFC, AFRAeS	14 June 1974
Gp. Capt. J.B. Duxbury MBE, ADC	5 June 1976
Gp. Capt. D.W. Hann	16 December 1977
Gp. Capt. C.J. Phillips	14 December 1979
Gp. Capt. A.A.G. Woodford BA, ADC	11 March 1982
Gp. Capt. R.G. Peters	15 December 1983
Gp. Capt. P.M. Stean	6 December 1985
Gp. Capt. C.T. Moore	18 March 1988
Gp. Capt. B.C. Laite	15 June 1990
Gp. Capt. S.J. Coy OBE	5 February 1993
Gp. Capt. M.R. Trace OBE, MA	2 March 1995

Section One

EARLY DAYS

DH84 Dragon G-ACMJ is pictured resting at Barnstaple while operating the daily Swansea–Barnstaple–Trebelzue–Penzance service of Western Airways, 8 May 1939.

Sir Alan Cobham, whose air display, the touring National Aviation Day Ltd, performed at Trebelzue during August 1933.

St Mawgan was always a popular station because of its proximity to holiday beaches. These St Mawgan-based WAAFs are pictured with a male companion at Newquay, 1944.

Newquay, June 1944, and Cpl. Cyphus relaxes with colleagues B. Thompson and F. Bianci.

Five KLM Douglas DC-3s escaped to England to join the BOAC fleet at Whitchurch, where this photograph was taken in 1940. Utilized on wartime routes, the aircraft flew via St Mawgan before crossing the Bay of Biscay en route to Lisbon.

A USAAF C-87A Liberator parked in front of St Mawgan's air traffic control tower, *c*. 1944. Note the line of eighteen Dakotas dispersed on the north side of the airfield.

An early picture showing Trebelzue with St Mawgan's main 32/14 runway dominating the airfield.

The ubiquitous Dakota could be found either operating from or visiting St Mawgan for nearly four decades. The squadron badge on this Danish C-47, pictured visiting St Mawgan during 1971, indicates that it was operated by 721 Squadron, Royal Danish Air Force.

No. 224 Squadron at Gibraltar operated Halifax Met.6s in the meteorological reconnaissance role. This example, ST804, is pictured at St Mawgan during November 1951, while returning to the UK and 48 MU at Hawarden. The Halifaxes of 224 Squadron had been replaced by Shackleton MR.1s, which were operated in the maritime reconnaissance role.

Lincoln B.1 RA648 parked at St Mawgan. Designed in 1943 to Air Ministry Specification B.14/43 as an improved Lancaster for the Pacific War, the Lincoln remained in RAF service until withdrawn from 151 Squadron, Signals Command, at RAF Watton on 12 March 1963.

A snow-covered St Mawgan, probably pictured in 1956.

Designed as a two-seat trainer, the Arado Ar 396 was developed at the SIPA works near Paris but was too late for German service. This postwar example was built for the French military and is pictured at Exeter in quasi-Luftwaffe colours during the summer of 1976, while en route to Trebelzue and the film set where it featured in the making of *The Eagle Has Landed*, starring Michael Caine among others.

Section Two

PERSONALITIES

A salute greets HM Queen Elizabeth II as she enters St Mawgan in the royal car, July 1966.

Sgt. Wallace, a WAAF nursing orderly at St Mawgan's sick quarters, 1944.

Personnel gathered outside St Mawgan's briefing room, a Nissen hut of wartime vintage.

A parade of St Mawgan-based WAAFs, Newquay, 1944. The Women's Auxiliary Air Force was constituted and formed from ATS units during 1939. Ten years later, in 1949, it became the Women's Royal Air Force, until disbanded and integrated into the RAF on 1 April 1994.

During the Second World War the ladies of the Women's Voluntary Service (WVS) assisted in the sergeants' mess at St Mawgan. This group photograph was taken in 1945; the mess provided a copy to each WVS helper.

Cpl. Cyphus with B. Thompson (right) and an unidentified individual, Newquay, June 1944. All three were members of the Air Despatch & Reception Unit (ADRU) at St Mawgan.

A trio of navigators from the SMR, winter 1952/3. From left to right: Johnny Chivers, Frank Amies, 'Ginger' Cockerell.

A trio of airmen pose in front of sonar buoys, June 1966. 'Nobby' Clarke (left) was in charge of the sonics bay, while Mick Davis (right) worked in sonics for some years. The third individual remains unidentified.

The old officers' mess bar, St Mawgan, 1951/2. From left to right: Flg. Offs. H. Bridle, T. Cullum. The identities of the bar steward and third mess member are unknown.

The AOC-in-C Strike Command, the late Sir Andrew Humphrey, and the station commander, Gp. Capt. P.M. Harvey (right), are about to enter the sergeants' mess, 3 March 1971.

Sir Andrew Humphrey talking to SWO WO McNaught, Flt. Sgt. (W(oman)) Bow, WO Piper and WO Bull.

National Service: SACs Bill Dobson (left) and Arthur Rookes at St Mawgan, 1957.

A mix of both Regular and National Servicemen pictured outside the carpenters' shop, *c.* 1957. The wooden object in the centre of the picture is a Punch & Judy stand that was being prepared for the annual Battle of Britain open day.

Sgt. Don Gilpin, personal assistant to St Mawgan's station commanders from 1968 to 1972.

SAC Bill Dobson pictured outside the carpenters' shop, *c.* 1957.

The carpenters' workshop, 1957. Left to right are Cpl. Jock Knotman, Alan Shears (National Service), the fabric worker, SAC John Nankival and SAC Arthur Rookes. In the front is LAC Norman Cook.

The interior of the carpenters' workshop. The timber rack contains various hardwoods, such as elm for aircraft chocks and de-icing strips, beech for internal joinery, ash for crates and repairs to bowser doors, and spruce (a softwood) for repairs to Anson aircraft, etc.

'Best blues' for a parade, either the AOC's inspection or the 'last of the Lancasters' parade, October 1956.

During his years as premier, the late Sir Harold Wilson regularly travelled through St Mawgan while en route to his Scillies holiday home. He is pictured at St Mawgan with the station commander, Gp. Capt. K.J. Barratt, on 18 August 1969.

Film star Elizabeth Taylor waiting outside the transit lounge at St Mawgan, 18 August 1969. She later welcomed a disabled 'End to End' competitor on arrival at Land's End from John O'Groats.

Section Three

LANCASTERS

Sgt. 'Taff' Caldwell poses with an SMR Lancaster, winter 1952/3.

The last Lancasters in front-line service were operated by 38 Squadron at Luqa, Malta. Here MR.3 RE221 'W' of 38 Squadron is pictured with its crew prior to heading for St Mawgan and retirement. During the summer of 1953, RE221 had located the crew of a Hastings that had ditched in the Mediterranean between Malta and Cyprus.

The very last front-line Lancaster, RF273 'T' of 38 Squadron, was photographed doing power checks at Luqa, before heading for St Mawgan and the breakers, February 1954.

Lancaster MR.3 SW367 remained in service with the SMR at St Mawgan until the type was withdrawn from second-line operations during the autumn of 1956.

Lancaster MR.3 RF311 was operated by the SMR from December 1955 until May 1956. It is pictured here at St Mawgan after a tail wheel collapse on 27 February 1956.

A sad-looking SMR Lancaster MR.3, pictured after an aborted take-off at St Mawgan.

RE159, a Lancaster MR.3 had previously served with the Luqa-based 37 and 38 Squadrons before joining the SMR at St Mawgan.

Battle of Britain Day, 19 September 1953. Cornwall vibrates to the mighty roar of forty-eight Rolls-Royce Merlin engines as the SMR parades its Lancasters. The French Naval Air Arm, the *Aéronavale*, also utilized ex-RAF Lancasters in the maritime reconnaissance role. Modified in the Avro plants at Woodford and Langar, provision was made in French Lancasters for the carriage of airborne lifeboats. Canadian Lancasters were also modified postwar and a number saw service with the RCAF in both the air-sea rescue and maritime reconnaissance roles.

A rear turret view of the 1953 Battle of Britain Day formation. The aircraft operated by the SMR were originally constructed as Lancaster B.IIIs. Subsequently they were sent to Eastleigh, Southampton, in July 1946, to be modified for air-sea rescue duties as ASR.3s, equipped with airborne lifeboats. They were then modified at a later date for maritime reconnaissance as GR.3s (later redesignated MR.3), initially with Packard Merlin 28 and 38 engines, but when these became obsolete, with Packard Merlin 224s.

Lancaster RF325 crosses the Cornish coast while participating in an air-to-air photo session for the St Mawgan Christmas card, 11 November 1953. The projection below the rear turret was the mounting for the rear-facing F24 camera utilized with electrically operated Very pistols loaded with photoflash cartridges to record low-level bombing results.

An air-to-air study of RE186, which had been operated by 236 OCU before joining the SMR at St Mawgan. Note the new dark grey colour scheme that was introduced by Coastal Command prior to retirement of the Lancaster.

St Mawgan as the last Lancaster, RF325, prepares to leave for the breakers, 15 October 1956. The American Air Rescue Service aircraft were searching for a US Navy R6D-1, missing with a full load of passengers since 10 October when en route from Lakenheath to the USA.

Pictured from the ATC tower, RF325 taxis to the runway for the last time.

Airborne for the last time, this picture of RF325 shows clearly that the earlier modification to ASR.III standard had included deletion of the dorsal turret.

RF325 on course for Wroughton with Wg. Cdr. E.J. Brookes at the controls: the era of the Lancaster in RAF service comes to an end. In a letter to A.V. Roe & Co. in December 1945, Marshal of the RAF Sir Arthur Harris GCB, OBE, AFC, LLD, Britain's wartime Commander-in-Chief of RAF Bomber Command, described the Lancaster as 'the greatest single factor in winning the war'. By the end of the war a total of 7,377 Lancasters had been built, with production peaking in August 1944, when a total of 293 aircraft were constructed.

Section Four

COURSES & CREWS

No. 220 Squadron's crew 4 poses in front of a Shackleton, October 1957. Aircraft Captain Flg. Off. Don Wimble is at the extreme left of the picture. The crew, previously captained by Flt. Sgt Pilot Jim Martin, had been Coastal Command's last fully senior NCO Shackleton crew.

The students of No. 54 Maritime Reconnaissance Course were photographed in front of an SMR Lancaster. The course was held at St Mawgan between July and November 1955.

No. 61 Maritime Reconnaissance Course was held at St Mawgan between March and June 1956.

SMR staff pilots, *c.* 1955. The CFI, Sqn. Ldr. F. Hazelwood, is fourth from right in the front row.

Section Five

SHACKLETONS

Shackleton T.4 WB822 of the MOTU pictured during a formation flyover of Cornwall's larger towns as an advertisement for the 1967 Battle of Britain air display.

Shackleton GR.1 VP289 pictured while receiving attention from the St Mawgan-based Coastal Command Modification Centre, 1951.

VP289 was one of twenty-nine Shackleton GR.1s from the first production batch of Shackletons that entered service with 120 Squadron and 236 OCU at Kinloss during February 1951.

Seen parked at a dispersal on the north side of the airfield, Shackleton T.4 WB849 clearly shows its MOTU ownership, September 1965.

Another MOTU Shackleton T.4, VP258, parked on the 'south' pan outside the large maintenance hangar, April 1968.

A trio of St Mawgan-based Shackletons head out to sea.

No. 204 Squadron was the only Coastal Command Shackleton squadron not to be based at St Mawgan. Between 1954 and 1972 the unit operated Shackleton MR.1As and MR.2s from Ballykelly and from 1971 at Honington.

Shackleton MR.2 WB826 of 220 Squadron is defuelled after a landing accident, 14 January 1957.

September 1965, and 201 Squadron's Shackleton MR.3 XF704 is dispersed on the north side of the airfield. All MR.3s eventually received Phase 2 and Phase 3 modifications that included diesel exhaust detection equipment to aid submarine location and the fitting of Viper 203 turbojets to boost take-off performance.

A No. 42 Squadron Shackleton MR.3 pictured subsequent to receiving full Phase 3 mods, September 1970.

Displayed in the static park at Chivenor's 1959 Battle of Britain air display, Shackleton MR.3 WR986 of 206 Squadron made the short flight up the coast from St Mawgan to add variety.

During late 1957, 220 Squadron converted to the Shackleton MR.3 and suffered a number of nose wheel collapses. Here the aircraft of crew 4, captained by Flg. Off. Don Wimble, comes to a stop in front of a crash crew, whose camera caught Sergeant Signaller Rex Perham making a hasty exit from the scene, with John Bussey leaving via the port escape hatch.

Another 220 Squadron nose wheel collapse. Nose down and with main wheel tyres smoking, the port escape hatch has already been opened to enable the crew to make a swift exit when the Shackleton stops.

A Shackleton MR.2 gets airborne from runway 31, *c.* 1964. The buildings in the foreground house the GCA facility; a visiting Meteor 8 and a pair of Chipmunk T.10s can be seen in the background.

Pictured in its normal working environment, this St Mawgan-based MR.3 Phase 3 clearly shows the Viper turbojet, installed in the rear of the starboard outer engine nacelle.

A fine study of a visiting Shackleton MR.2 from 204 Squadron. This example, WR966, was later converted to MR.2(T) standard.

The South African Air Force received eight Shackleton MR.3s from the initial production batch. The first two examples, including 176 (illustrated), were deployed to St Mawgan during the summer of 1957 for crew training.

On 1 October 1958, 220 Squadron at St Mawgan was renumbered 201 and flew Shackleton MR.3s for the next twelve years. In March 1965 the Squadron moved to Scotland where it converted to Nimrods in October 1970.

A Shackleton MR.3 of 206 Squadron crosses the Cornish coast near St Mawgan.

On Thursday 23 September 1971, the last St Mawgan-based Shackleton, XF703 of 42 Squadron, left the station for RAF Henlow and the custody of the Royal Air Force Museum. The picture depicts the senior airman of each trade, before take-off. Centre in the front row is Chief Technician John Beal BEM.

No. 42 Squadron's ground crew with the last Shackleton before its departure.

St Mawgan's last Shackleton was photographed by Stuart Roberts, who as the longest serving airman at St Mawgan was rewarded with the task of marshalling out the last St Mawgan-based Shackleton.

With Welshman Flt. Lt. Colin Hughes at the controls, XF703 lifts from the runway for the last time.

Section Six

MISCELLANEOUS RAF UNITS

On 1 February 1958, 217 Squadron was re-formed at St Mawgan from No. 1360 Flight. The squadron moved to Christmas Island on 14 February as part of a combined force supporting the nuclear trials being carried out there. Illustrated at St Mawgan is a 217 Squadron Whirlwind HAR.2, XJ762.

Bristol 171 Sycamore HR.12 WV781, the first of a trials batch of four for Coastal Command that were operated by the ASWDU at St Mawgan.

A ladder dangles precariously beneath Sycamore HR.12 WV784, apparently while undergoing ASWDU trials at St Mawgan, 1951/2. WV784 was redesigned to carry sonar, with a crew of two for trials purposes.

In the hover at St Mawgan are three ASWDU Sycamore HR.12s from the Coastal Command trials batch.

Used experimentally by the ASWDU, Shackleton MR.2 WL789 was flown at St Mawgan during 1954 with a MAD (Magnetic Anomaly Detection) 'stinger' tail.

Vickers Varsity T.1 WF330 carried Coastal Command titles and ranged far and wide on communications duties. It is pictured close to home at Exeter on 1 September 1959.

Martlesham Heath, 21 April 1960. Varsity WF330 waits for its return flight to St Mawgan.

Winter sunshine, 23 February 1971. A pair of Training Command Varsities is pictured on a visit to St Mawgan.

Varsity T.1 WJ897 sits on a wet apron while visiting St Mawgan, 22 January 1969.

Anson C.19 TX222 of 19 Group Communications Flight was later written off when it collided with trees in bad visibility at Botley Hill, Titsey, Surrey, 14 August 1957.

Transport Command Anson C.21 VS572 carries code letters indicating ownership by the Northolt-based Metropolitan Communications Squadron.

This locally built BE.2c replica, pictured at St Mawgan on 4 August 1976, represents the First World War biplane that served in France with the Royal Flying Corps in the reconnaissance, artillery-spotting and bombing roles. The BE.2c also served with the Home Defence squadrons, achieving considerable combat success against Zeppelins.

Search & Rescue facilities at St Mawgan were introduced when 'A' Flight of 22 Squadron became operational at the station during June 1956. Whirlwind HAR.4 XJ407 is illustrated.

No. 7 Squadron was re-formed at St Mawgan on 1 May 1970 to provide target facilities for Army and Navy units throughout the UK. A Canberra TT.18 is pictured holding formation off the starboard wing of the Nimrod photo-plane.

Section Seven

VISITING MILITARY AIRCRAFT

French Air Force Nord 2501F Noratles No. 162 is visiting St Mawgan, autumn 1964. It is of similar twin-boom configuration to the Fairchild C-82 and C-119 Flying Boxcar. With some 425 examples built in France and Germany, the Noratles was also used by the air forces of West Germany, Israel, Greece and Niger.

A PBY-5A Catalina amphibian of No. 333 *Skv*, Royal Norwegian Air Force. The Catalina saw widespread use during the Second World War as a long-range patrol and rescue amphibian. Postwar, the Catalina featured world-wide in the air-sea rescue role. The last in service with Latin American air forces were retired in 1965–6.

Bundesmarine Grumman G-191 Albatross 6008 is pictured visiting St Mawgan, 18 August 1970. West German Albatrosses last served with a *staffel* of *Marinefliegergeschwader* 5 (MFG5) before being sold as surplus in 1972.

A permanent USAF Search & Rescue facility was set up at Manston from April 1951 with the arrival of the 9th Air Rescue Squadron operating SA-16 Albatross and SB-29 Flying Fortress aircraft. Expanded in November 1953, the unit was redesignated the 66th Air Rescue Squadron. Albatross 51-5287 is pictured refuelling at St Mawgan.

The Royal Norwegian Air Force received a total of twenty SHU-16B ASW amphibians to equip *Skv* 330 at Bodo and *Skv* 333 at Andoya, which remained in service until 1969. This *Skv* 333 example was visiting St Mawgan.

Seen here at St Mawgan, this SHU-16B was from *Skv* 330 at Bodo. Formed as the RAF's 330 Squadron on 25 April 1941 with Norwegian naval personnel, the squadron moved to Norway after the German surrender, under Royal Norwegian Air Force control.

DHC-built CS2F-2 Tracker 1578 is pictured visiting St Mawgan, 18 September 1969. Licence-built in Canada, the Grumman design was operated by Shearwater-based VS-880 and VS-881 of the Canadian Armed Forces. The two squadrons shared responsibility for providing eight-aircraft detachments aboard HMCS *Bonaventure* until the last Tracker was launched on 12 December 1969 and the carrier retired.

Visiting St Mawgan is West German Air Force Convair 440 12-06, 18 September 1969. Ex-airline Convair 440s also served with the Bolivian, Italian and Spanish air forces.

A Douglas C-121A Globemaster II, modified to C-124C standard and operated by Military Airlift Command's 445th Military Airlift Wing, visits St Mawgan, 25 March 1969.

Mildenhall's C-1A Trader visiting St Mawgan, summer 1975.

The air search for a missing US transport aircraft off the Azores centres on St Mawgan, *c.* 1955. A pair of Air Rescue Service SC-54Ds shares the tarmac with 51-7259, the last production KC-97F. The S2F and TF1 on the right of the picture had arrived with aircraft debris retrieved from the sea in the search area.

The Chilean Air Force operated a mixture of six Douglas DC-6A/Bs. Based at Los Cerrillos, Santiago, and operated by *Grupo* 10, this example pictured visiting St Mawgan was formerly N90772 in US airline service and was subsequently written off in an accident on 24 July 1977.

This US Navy Lockheed P2V-5 Neptune, BuNo. 131417, was operated by VP-44 and based at NAS Brunswick, Maine, when deployed at St Mawgan.

This Royal Netherlands Navy SP-2H Neptune, based at Volkenburg with 320 Squadron, is seen visiting St Mawgan. Dutch Neptunes were regular visitors to Cornwall.

Dutch SP–2H Neptune 203 was one of fifteen P2V-7Bs delivered between September 1961 and February 1962. With four 20 mm cannon in a metal nose, they were operated by 321 Squadron against Indonesia, out of Biak, New Guinea.

In 1962 Dutch Neptunes were modified to SP-2H standard with glazed nose, and then assigned to Valkenburg for operational duties.

France was the largest foreign recipient of Lockheed-built Neptunes, taking thirty-one P2V-6s in 1953 and a further thirty-four P2V-7s in subsequent years. The Neptunes were frequent visitors to St Mawgan and remained in service until 1984, when *Escadrille* 12S was re-equipped with Dassault Gardians.

The longevity of the Neptune in French service is illustrated by P2V-7 147567, which contrasts with the high-tech Nimrod parked in the background at St Mawgan, March 1981.

A fine study of a visiting French Neptune at St Mawgan. A number were modified to operate in support of the French atomic test and missile programmes and based at Tahiti-Faaa in French Polynesia. Six aircraft underwent modification that included the installation of missile-tracking equipment in the nose.

Twenty-five P2V-7s built to a special configuration, initially without underwing jet pods, were delivered to the RCAF during 1955. Subsequently, jet pods were fitted; they can be clearly seen under the port wing of this Canadian example visiting St Mawgan.

In Canadian service the Neptune was operated by 404, 405 and 407 Squadrons, remaining in service until the early 1970s when they were replaced by the Canadair CP-107 Argus. Many were then used by civilian operators in North America for fire-fighting.

A mixed bag of front-line maritime patrol aircraft. From left to right: Avro Shackleton MR.3, Lockheed SP-2H Neptune, Canadair CL-28 Argus, HS Nimrod, Lockheed P-3 Orion. The aircraft were probably participating in a maritime exercise that centred on St Mawgan.

The Canadair CL-288 Argus (military designation CP-107) was designed to meet a 1952 requirement for a maritime aircraft to replace the Avro Lancaster MR.10 and Lockheed P2V Neptune with the RCAF's Maritime Air Command. This example carries the insignia of one of the Greenwood-based squadrons, VP405.

Visiting St Mawgan during May 1960, Argus 20740 was operated by VP-449, the training unit. The Argus fleet was grounded during 1972 because of landing gear problems, but remained in service until the end of 1981.

This Lockheed P-3K Orion of the Royal New Zealand Air Force, together with its crew, was the winner of the Fincastle Trophy competition held at St Mawgan, October 1980.

VP-26 based at Brunswick, Maine, a component of the Atlantic Fleet's Patrol Wing 5 (PATWING 5), operated P-3C Orions when this example visited St Mawgan during the Fincastle Trophy Competition, 1980.

The P-3C Orion-equipped VP-47 operated from NAS Jacksonville, Florida, and sent this example to participate in St Mawgan-based exercises, 1975.

A Lockheed P-3A Orion of VP-30, the Jacksonville-based East Coast training squadron. Aircraft from this unit were regular visitors to the RAF's maritime stations. The Orion illustrated was written off on 18 January 1981.

The US Naval Oceanographic Office P-3 Orion *Arctic Fox* was utilized for '*Project Birdseye*', frequently visiting the UK including, in this instance, St Mawgan.

In Canadian service the Lockheed P-3 Orion was designated the CP-140 Aurora, entering service during 1980 when it replaced the CP-107 Argus. This Aurora from VP-404 at Greenwood is seen at St Mawgan on 10 October 1980.

The Royal Netherlands naval air service were regular visitors to St Mawgan during the 1970s, frequently participating in exercises in the Western Approaches. Breguet Atlantic (SP-13A) 250 was the first of ten delivered to the Dutch.

The French naval air arm, the *Aéronavale*, also operated a fleet of Atlantics, from bases at Nîmes-Garons and Lann Bihoué. This example, again pictured at St Mawgan, was from the initial batch of four prototypes and sixty-nine production aircraft.

Section Eight

NIMRODS & CANBERRAS

The newly formed 236 OCU received the first of its new Hawker Siddeley Nimrod MR.1s during October 1969, enabling the Nimrod to make its public debut in Cornwall just eleven months later at the Battle of Britain air display, 18 September 1970.

This well-known PR picture highlights the close affinity between St Mawgan and Newquay, as Nimrod MR.1 XV234 flies along the coast with Newquay in the background.

This is the fourth production Nimrod, XV229, in its natural maritime environment. From 1977 Nimrod MR.1 aircraft were progressively updated to Nimrod MR.2 standard by the installation of more sophisticated electronic equipment.

With their long-range and maritime role, the St Mawgan-based Nimrods ranged far and wide. Here Nimrod MR.1 XZ282 is pictured at NAS Point Mugu, California, positioned in front of the crowd line before participating in the flying display.

The Nimrod starts its flying display at Point Mugu. An important West Coast base, Point Mugu is also home to the Pacific Missile Range.

The large hangar which dominates St Mawgan was constructed for the Nimrod. The size of the building is apparent from the hangared aircraft.

The affinity of St Mawgan with the Nimrod ended in 1992 when 42 Squadron moved to Scotland to join the Kinloss Maritime Wing. Nimrod MR.2P is shown here during a flying display at RAF Abingdon, 15 September 1990. The in-flight refuelling probe installed as a result of the Falklands War can be clearly seen over the nose of the aeroplane.

An insight into the important role that would be played by the Canberras of 7 Squadron was provided by Boscombe Down's Aircraft & Armament Evaluation Establishment (A&AEE) which exhibited modified Canberra B.2 WH876 at St Mawgan's Battle of Britain air display, September 1966. The Canberra was engaged in development flying with a variety of towed targets.

The Canberra TT.18 was the definitive target tug version of the former RAF bomber, with this 7 Squadron example pictured while parked at St Mawgan, autumn 1971.

Over St Mawgan a 7 Squadron Canberra TT.18 hauls a sleeve target.

A superb air-to-air study of a camouflaged Canberra TT.18 of 7 Squadron, whose insignia is painted above the fin flash. The front of the port winch is clearly visible, under the leading edge of the wing.

Section Nine

AIR DAY VISITORS

With 'south pan' acting as the static aircraft park, the spectators begin to assemble on the crowd line for an air day, 1960s.

Visitors mingle in front of the air traffic control tower, always at the hub of air day operations.

Slim and purposeful Spitfire 19 PS853, originally delivered to No. 1 PRU at Benson on 13 January 1945 and subsequently operated by the Battle of Britain Memorial Flight, waits for the runway before starting its display routine at St Mawgan.

The Vickers Valiant was the first of the 'V' class four-jet bombers to enter squadron service. Valiant WZ382, a B(PR)K.1 from 543 Squadron at Wyton, taxis from St Mawgan's static park, September 1964.

The Avro Vulcan was the second of the 'V' class bombers to enter service. No. 9 Squadron exhibited its Vulcan B.2 XM653 at St Mawgan's Battle of Britain air display on 18 September 1965.

The Victor was the last of three new types ordered for the RAF under the 'V' bomber programme. This B.1, XA936, operated by 232 OCU, was subsequently converted for in-flight refuelling operations as a BK.1 and is pictured leaving the static park after the 1965 air display.

With drab camouflage replacing the early anti-flash overall white finish of the early 'V' bombers, Handley Page Victor K.1A XH590 from 55 Squadron at Marham graces the static aircraft park at St Mawgan, 18 September 1971.

A Victor K.1A from 55 Squadron also featured in the 1971 flying display, providing a demonstation of flight-refuelling operations with a pair of Binbrook-based Lightning F.6s from 11 Squadron.

The Gloster Javelin, the first twin-jet delta fighter in the world, entered service with the RAF in February 1956. RAF Germany sent this FAW9, XH769, from 11 Squadron at Geilenkirchen for St Mawgan's air day on 19 September 1964.

This 'Project Magnet' NC-121K, BuNo. 145924, *El Coyote*, was the star of St Mawgan's static display, 19 September 1964.

From 1950 until 1955, the Meteor F.8 was the major single-seat day interceptor with Fighter Command. Re-designated TT.8, a number continued to serve on target-towing duties, 229 OCU at Chivenor providing WK941 for the 1964 static display.

Reflecting the setting sun, North American F-100D Super Sabre 55-3684 taxis from the static park, 19 September 1964.

Armée de l'Air Super Mystère B2 No. 132 carried the unit markings of *Escadron* EC1/12 'Cambresis' based at Cambrai, when it was photographed in the static park at St Mawgan on 19 September 1964.

Watton-based Varsity T.1 WL691 of 115 Squadron displayed in the static park, 19 September 1964.

The Hunter F.6 first entered service in 1956, replacing earlier variants of the fighter. The F.6, later relegated to second-line roles, was represented by XF386 from 229 OCU at Chivenor when displayed in the static park at St Mawgan on 18 September 1965.

United States Air Forces in Europe (USAFE) provided a pair of F-101A Voodoos from the 81st Tactical Fighter Wing (TFW) at Bentwaters/Woodbridge for the static park at the 1965 air day on 18 September.

A second photograph, taken from a different angle, shows clearly the colourful tail markings of the 81st TFW. This unit was the only wing to operate the dedicated fighter variant of the Voodoo outside the USA.

The RCAF provided Lockheed P2V-7 Neptune 24122 for static display, 18 September 1965. Maritime Air Command operated the Neptune as a 'stop-gap' between the Lancaster and the Argus.

On 12 May 1965 the first RF-4C Phantom joined the 10th Tactical Reconnaissance Wing at Alconbury. Sufficient re-equipment had taken place to enable the American unit to provide this grey and white painted example for static display in September 1966.

Compared with the top photograph on p. 103, the application of camouflage paint to the USAFE F-100 Super Sabre fleet is apparent, having been done before St Mawgan's 1966 air day in September.

For the 1966 air day on 17 September, the A&AEE at Boscombe Down provided North American Harvard II KF183. Although retaining the overall yellow trainer colours, the Harvard was operated at Boscombe Down for low-speed photographic and calibration duties, remaining in service during 1995.

The 1971 air day on 18 September enabled 42 Squadron's last Shackleton MR.3, XF703, to make a final public curtain call, with retirement taking place just five days later on 23 September.

The work-horse of air forces and airlines world-wide for nearly sixty years, the DC-3 or C-47 Dakota is illustrated by Royal Danish Air Force C-47A K-683, operated by 721 Squadron and displayed statically at the same air day.

Always a show-stopper, the Battle of Britain Memorial Flight's airworthy Lancaster, PA474, is one of only two surviving flying examples, out of a total of 7,377 Lancasters built. It is pictured before taking part in the 1971 air day.

Night fighter variants of the Gloster Meteor were developed and produced by Gloster's sister company, Armstrong Whitworth Aircraft. NF.11 WD790 was modified to NF.12 standards, with extra fin area and a longer nose. It was delivered to Ferranti for radar trials and appeared in the static park for the air day on behalf of the RSRE at Pershore.

No. 321 Squadron of the Royal Netherlands naval air service provided this Valkenburg-based Atlantic for the 1971 air day.

In line astern, a trio of Varsity T.1s from No. 6 Flying Training School at Finningley overfly St Mawgan at the air day.

CF-104 Starfighter 104891 was one of 200 aircraft manufactured by Canadair under a contract awarded by the Canadian Government on 24 July 1959. Based at Baden-Sollingen as part of a three-squadron wing deployed by Canadian Forces Europe, the Starfighter is pictured leaving the static park at the conclusion of the 1971 air day.

A traditional Handley Page heavyweight, Hastings T.1 TG568 is about to become airborne at the air day.

The Royal Aircraft Establishment's Farnborough-based Gloster Meteor T.7 XF274 on the runway during the 1971 air day. The Meteor was subsequently destroyed in an accident at Farnborough.

The Lockheed Orion, the West's most important land-based anti-submarine patrol aircraft, was represented at the air day by US Navy P-3B BuNo. 153446 from VP-11.

St Mawgan supplied this 206 Squadron Shackleton MR.3 for display at a Chivenor open day, *c.* 1959.

Hunter FGA.9 XE552 from 229 OCU at Chivenor carried the markings of 79 (Reserve) Squadron when it appeared on the static park for St Mawgan's 1972 air day.

The Red Arrows have earned acclaim as the RAF's premier aerobatic team. The red-painted Gnat T.1s frequently appeared at St Mawgan, flown by instructors of the Central Flying School. In 1979 the BAe Hawk superseded the Gnat.

Star turn at the 1976 air day was this Short Sandringham flying boat of Antilles Air Boats. Operating from its summer charter base at Foynes, the big flying boat was flown by its owner, Capt. Blair, accompanied by his wife, film star Maureen O'Hara.

Section Ten

FAST JETS

The English Electric (later BAC) Lightning was the first single-seat RAF fighter to exceed the speed of sound in level flight. Lightning F.3 XR750 of 226 OCU's 2(T) Squadron is pictured a split second after becoming airborne from St Mawgan's runway.

Lightning F.1A XM188 from 226 OCU, which trained Lightning pilots at Coltishall, visited St Mawgan for the 1964 air day. The picture illustrates the use of 145 Squadron's designation and shadow squadron unit markings.

The most colourful of all Lightnings were those of 226 OCU. With a red spine and fin, and a white rudder and inset which entered the red fin area, the colours are well illustrated on the unit's two-seat Lightning T.4 XM996, which also attended the 1964 air day.

Lightning F.3 XP753 of the Lightning Training Flight was the official flying display Lightning in 1983. It is pictured during an impressive take-off routine at St Mawgan.

This photograph shows the purposeful lines of Lightning F.3 XR749, which carries the red-and-white chequerboard markings and Phoenix fin crest of 56 Squadron. The chequerboard markings date from the unit's pre-war colour scheme.

Always an impressive air-display performer, in this instance a Lightning F.3 from 5 Squadron at Binbrook opens its display at St Mawgan. The unit badge on the fin combines '5' with a red maple leaf on a circular white field.

This is a North American F-100 Super Sabre, the first of the USAF's Century-series fighters and the world's first operational fighter capable of level supersonic performance. UK-based units operating the F-100 were the 20th TFW at Wethersfield (later Upper Heyford) and the 48th TFW at Lakenheath.

The McDonnell RF-101C, the dedicated reconnaissance variant of the Voodoo, equipped the 66th Tactical Reconnaisance Wing (TRW) at Upper Heyford between August 1966 and 1969. This RF-101C is pictured in the static park at St Mawgan.

Destined to become the USA's most significant fighter of the 1960s and 1970s, the McDonnell Douglas F-4 Phantom II was represented by the F-4J variant when US Marine Corps fighter squadron VMFA-122, nicknamed 'The Crusaders', staged through St Mawgan.

VMFA-122's F-4J BuNo. 157243. The unit was normally based at the Marine Corps Air Station at Beaufort, South Carolina, but took its Phantoms to war in Vietnam, frequently flying close support missions in support of ground forces.

The 10th TRW at Alconbury converted to the reconnaissance version of the Phantom, the RF-4C, during 1965. Succeeding the RF-101 in the tactical reconnaissance role, the Rf-4C carried cameras in the nose, together with sideways-looking radar and an infra-red line scanner in the fuselage. In this picture the undercarriage of the RF-4C is starting to retract after take-off at St Mawgan.

The Phantom FG.1 entered service with the RAF in September 1969, in the air defence interceptor role, the FGR.2 following in the ground attack and tactical reconnaissance role twelve months later. Here a Phantom FG.1 from 43 Squadron at Leuchars is pictured seconds after take-off from St. Mawgan.

With the entry into service of the Jaguar as the RAF's principal tactical ground-attack aircraft, Phantom FGR.2s began to revert to the pure interceptor role. This 56 Squadron example from Wattisham is pictured on 'south' pan at St Mawgan.

Developed as an air-superiority fighter for the USAF's Tactical Air Command, the Lockheed F-104 Starfighter was operated by some fourteen overseas air forces including Italy. This Italian F-104C was being operated by the 36° *Stormo* at Gioia del Colle when it visited St Mawgan.

This photograph brings St Mawgan's fast-jet story up to date and illustrates the longevity of the F-104 Starfighter. With improved radar, air-to-air missiles and modern ECM systems, this F-104S was being operated by 10° *Gruppo* of 9° *Stormo* at Grazzanise when it visited St Mawgan on 3 August 1993.

Section Eleven

NEWQUAY AIRPORT

The opening of the Starways service to Liverpool in 1959 heralded attempts by a variety of operators to introduce regular Newquay-London services. Westpoint Airlines was formed at Exeter in 1961 and used the ubiquitous Dakota on routes out of the West Country. This is Dakota G-AMDB at Newquay, August 1965.

After the demise of Westpoint in 1965, British Midland Airways re-established the Newquay–London route. Here the airline's Dakota G-AOGZ waits for passengers at Newquay's small civil air terminal, July 1966.

Dakota G-ANTD in full British Midland Airways livery at Newquay, June 1966.

Operated by Intra of Jersey, Dakota G-AMPO is seen here parked outside the civil air terminal, August 1976.

In 1977 Brymon Airways took over the London route. The mainstay was Herald G-ATIG. The regularity of the Brymon operation resulted in the current four-times daily Newquay–London service being operated in British Airways livery and with a style of onboard service consistent with that of British Airways.

Acknowledgements

Thanks for the loan of pictures, background information and other help are due to:

D. Acland • R.C.B. Ashworth • W. Batty • L. Brown • J.E. Bussey
W. Cockerell • B. Cole • G.W. (Tony) Cullum • D.C. Elliott • D. Fowkes
D. Gilpin • D. Green • J. Gregory • M.E. Huntley • R.T. Jackson
G. Mudford • Revd. I.S. Partridge • the late G. Raby • S. Roberts • A. Rookes
Flt. Lt. A.S. Thomas RAF • B. Thompson • Sqn. Ldr. J.R. Wilson RAF

Members of the Liskeard Squadron of the Air Training Corps, pictured while attending summer camp at St Mawgan. The exact date is unknown, but was sometime between 1952 and 1956.

BRITAIN IN OLD PHOTOGRAPHS

To order any of these titles please telephone Littlehampton Book Services on 01903 721596

ALDERNEY

Alderney: A Second Selection, *B Bonnard*

BEDFORDSHIRE

Bedfordshire at Work, *N Lutt*

BERKSHIRE

Maidenhead, *M Hayles & D Hedges*
Around Maidenhead, *M Hayles & B Hedges*
Reading, *P Southerton*
Reading: A Second Selection, *P Southerton*
Sandhurst and Crowthorne, *K Dancy*
Around Slough, *J Hunter & K Hunter*
Around Thatcham, *P Allen*
Around Windsor, *B Hedges*

BUCKINGHAMSHIRE

Buckingham and District, *R Cook*
High Wycombe, *R Goodearl*
Around Stony Stratford, *A Lambert*

CHESHIRE

Cheshire Railways, *M Hitches*
Chester, *S Nichols*

CLWYD

Clwyd Railways, *M Hitches*

CLYDESDALE

Clydesdale, *Lesmahagow Parish Historical Association*

CORNWALL

Cornish Coast, *T Bowden*
Falmouth, *P Gilson*
Lower Fal, *P Gilson*
Around Padstow, *M McCarthy*
Around Penzance, *J Holmes*
Penzance and Newlyn, *J Holmes*
Around Truro, *A Lyne*
Upper Fal, *P Gilson*

CUMBERLAND

Cockermouth and District, *J Bernard Bradbury*
Keswick and the Central Lakes, *J Marsh*
Around Penrith, *F Boyd*
Around Whitehaven, *H Fancy*

DERBYSHIRE

Derby, *D Buxton*
Around Matlock, *D Barton*

DEVON

Colyton and Seaton, *T Gosling*
Dawlish and Teignmouth, *G Gosling*
Devon Aerodromes, *K Saunders*
Exeter, *P Thomas*
Exmouth and Budleigh Salterton, *T Gosling*
From Haldon to Mid-Dartmoor, *T Hall*
Honiton and the Otter Valley, *J Yallop*
Around Kingsbridge, *K Tanner*
Around Seaton and Sidmouth, *T Gosling*
Seaton, Axminster and Lyme Regis, *T Gosling*

DORSET

Around Blandford Forum, *B Cox*
Bournemouth, *M Colman*
Bridport and the Bride Valley, *J Burrell & S Humphries*
Dorchester, *T Gosling*
Around Gillingham, *P Crocker*

DURHAM

Darlington, *G Flynn*
Darlington: A Second Selection, *G Flynn*
Durham People, *M Richardson*
Houghton-le-Spring and Hetton-le-Hole, *K Richardson*
Houghton-le-Spring and Hetton-le-Hole: A Second Selection, *K Richardson*
Sunderland, *S Miller & B Bell*
Teesdale, *D Coggins*
Teesdale: A Second Selection, *P Raine*
Weardale, *J Crosby*
Weardale: A Second Selection, *J Crosby*

DYFED

Aberystwyth and North Ceredigion, *Dyfed Cultural Services Dept*
Haverfordwest, *Dyfed Cultural Services Dept*
Upper Tywi Valley, *Dyfed Cultural Services Dept*

ESSEX

Around Grays, *B Evans*

GLOUCESTERSHIRE

Along the Avon from Stratford to Tewkesbury, *J Jeremiah*
Cheltenham: A Second Selection, *R Whiting*
Cheltenham at War, *P Gill*
Cirencester, *J Welsford*
Around Cirencester, *E Cuss & P Griffiths*
Forest, The, *D Mullin*
Gloucester, *J Voyce*
Around Gloucester, *A Sutton*
Gloucester: From the Walwin Collection, *J Voyce*
North Cotswolds, *D Viner*
Severn Vale, *A Sutton*
Stonehouse to Painswick, *A Sutton*
Stroud and the Five Valleys, *S Gardiner & L Padin*
Stroud and the Five Valleys: A Second Selection, *S Gardiner & L Padin*
Stroud's Golden Valley, *S Gardiner & L Padin*
Stroudwater and Thames & Severn Canals, *E Cuss & S Gardiner*
Stroudwater and Thames & Severn Canals: A Second Selection, *E Cuss & S Gardiner*
Tewkesbury and the Vale of Gloucester, *C Hilton*
Thornbury to Berkeley, *J Hudson*
Uley, Dursley and Cam, *A Sutton*
Wotton-under-Edge to Chipping Sodbury, *A Sutton*

GWYNEDD

Anglesey, *M Hitches*
Gwynedd Railways, *M Hitches*
Around Llandudno, *M Hitches*
Vale of Conwy, *M Hitches*

HAMPSHIRE

Gosport, *J Sadden*
Portsmouth, *P Rogers & D Francis*

HEREFORDSHIRE

Herefordshire, *A Sandford*

HERTFORDSHIRE

Barnet, *I Norrie*
Hitchin, *A Fleck*
St Albans, *S Mullins*
Stevenage, *M Appleton*

ISLE OF MAN

The Tourist Trophy, *B Snelling*

ISLE OF WIGHT

Newport, *D Parr*
Around Ryde, *D Parr*

JERSEY

Jersey: A Third Selection, *R Lemprière*

KENT

Bexley, *M Scott*
Broadstairs and St Peter's, *J Whyman*
Bromley, Keston and Hayes, *M Scott*
Canterbury: A Second Selection, *D Butler*
Chatham and Gillingham, *P MacDougall*
Chatham Dockyard, *P MacDougall*
Deal, *J Broady*
Early Broadstairs and St Peter's, *B Wootton*
East Kent at War, *D Collyer*
Eltham, *J Kennett*
Folkestone: A Second Selection, *A Taylor & E Rooney*
Goudhurst to Tenterden, *A Guilmant*
Gravesend, *R Hiscock*
Around Gravesham, *R Hiscock & D Grierson*
Herne Bay, *J Hawkins*
Lympne Airport, *D Collyer*
Maidstone, *I Hales*
Margate, *R Clements*
RAF Hawkinge, *R Humphreys*
RAF Manston, *RAF Manston History Club*
RAF Manston: A Second Selection, *RAF Manston History Club*
Ramsgate and Thanet Life, *D Perkins*
Romney Marsh, *E Carpenter*
Sandwich, *C Wanostrocht*
Around Tonbridge, *C Bell*
Tunbridge Wells, *M Rowlands & I Beavis*
Tunbridge Wells: A Second Selection, *M Rowlands & I Beavis*
Around Whitstable, *C Court*
Wingham, Adisham and Littlebourne, *M Crane*

LANCASHIRE

Around Barrow-in-Furness, *J Garbutt & J Marsh*
Blackpool, *C Rothwell*
Bury, *J Hudson*
Chorley and District, *J Smith*
Fleetwood, *C Rothwell*
Heywood, *J Hudson*
Around Kirkham, *C Rothwell*
Lancashire North of the Sands, *J Garbutt & J Marsh*
Around Lancaster, *S Ashworth*
Lytham St Anne's, *C Rothwell*
North Fylde, *C Rothwell*
Radcliffe, *J Hudson*
Rossendale, *B Moore & N Dunnachie*

LEICESTERSHIRE

Around Ashby-de-la-Zouch, *K Hillier*
Charnwood Forest, *I Keil, W Humphrey & D Wix*
Leicester, *D Burton*
Leicester: A Second Selection, *D Burton*
Melton Mowbray, *T Hickman*
Around Melton Mowbray, *T Hickman*
River Soar, *D Wix, P Shacklock & I Keil*
Rutland, *T Clough*
Vale of Belvoir, *T Hickman*
Around the Welland Valley, *S Mastoris*

LINCOLNSHIRE

Grimsby, *J Tierney*
Around Grimsby, *J Tierney*
Grimsby Docks, *J Tierney*
Lincoln, *D Cuppleditch*

Scunthorpe, *D Taylor*
Skegness, *W Kime*
Around Skegness, *W Kime*

LONDON

Balham and Tooting, *P Loobey*
Crystal Palace, Penge & Anerley, *M Scott*
Greenwich and Woolwich, *K Clark*
Hackney: A Second Selection, *D Mander*
Lewisham and Deptford, *J Coulter*
Lewisham and Deptford: A Second Selection, *J Coulter*
Streatham, *P Loobey*
Around Whetstone and North Finchley, *J Heathfield*
Woolwich, *B Evans*

MONMOUTHSHIRE

Chepstow and the River Wye, *A Rainsbury*
Monmouth and the River Wye, *Monmouth Museum*

NORFOLK

Great Yarmouth, *M Teun*
Norwich, *M Colman*
Wymondham and Attleborough, *P Yaxley*

NORTHAMPTONSHIRE

Around Stony Stratford, *A Lambert*

NOTTINGHAMSHIRE

Arnold and Bestwood, *M Spick*
Arnold and Bestwood: A Second Selection, *M Spick*
Changing Face of Nottingham, *G Oldfield*
Mansfield, *Old Mansfield Society*
Around Newark, *T Warner*
Nottingham: 1944–1974, *D Whitworth*
Sherwood Forest, *D Ottewell*
Victorian Nottingham, *M Payne*

OXFORDSHIRE

Around Abingdon, *P Horn*
Banburyshire, *M Barnett & S Gosling*
Burford, *A Jewell*
Around Didcot and the Hagbournes, *B Lingham*
Garsington, *M Gunther*
Around Henley-on-Thames, *S Ellis*
Oxford: The University, *J Rhodes*
Thame to Watlington, *N Hood*
Around Wallingford, *D Beasley*
Witney, *T Worley*
Around Witney, *C Mitchell*
Witney District, *T Worley*
Around Woodstock, *J Bond*

POWYS

Brecon, *Brecknock Museum*
Welshpool, *E Bredsdorff*

SHROPSHIRE

Shrewsbury, *D Trumper*
Whitchurch to Market Drayton, *M Morris*

SOMERSET

Bath, *J Hudson*
Bridgwater and the River Parrett, *R Fitzhugh*
Bristol, *D Moorcroft & N Campbell-Sharp*
Changing Face of Keynsham,
B Lowe & M Whitehead
Chard and Ilminster, *G Gosling & F Huddy*
Crewkerne and the Ham Stone Villages,
G Gosling & F Huddy
Around Keynsham and Saltford, *B Lowe & T Brown*
Midsomer Norton and Radstock, *C Howell*
Somerton, Ilchester and Langport, *G Gosling & F Huddy*
Taunton, *N Chipchase*
Around Taunton, *N Chipchase*
Wells, *C Howell*
Weston-Super-Mare, *S Poole*
Around Weston-Super-Mare, *S Poole*
West Somerset Villages, *K Houghton & L Thomas*

STAFFORDSHIRE

Aldridge, *J Farrow*
Bilston, *E Rees*
Black Country Transport: Aviation, *A Brew*
Around Burton upon Trent, *G Sowerby & R Farman*
Bushbury, *A Chatwin, M Mills & E Rees*
Around Cannock, *M Mills & S Belcher*
Around Leek, *R Poole*
Lichfield, *H Clayton & K Simmons*
Around Pattingham and Wombourne, *M Griffiths, P Leigh & M Mills*
Around Rugeley, *T Randall & J Anslow*
Smethwick, *J Maddison*
Stafford, *J Anslow & T Randall*
Around Stafford, *J Anslow & T Randall*
Stoke-on-Trent, *I Lawley*
Around Tamworth, *R Sulima*
Around Tettenhall and Codsall, *M Mills*
Tipton, Wednesbury and Darlaston, *R Pearson*
Walsall, *D Gilbert & M Lewis*
Wednesbury, *I Bott*
West Bromwich, *R Pearson*

SUFFOLK

Ipswich: A Second Selection, *D Kindred*
Around Ipswich, *D Kindred*
Around Mildenhall, *C Dring*
Southwold to Aldeburgh, *H Phelps*
Around Woodbridge, *H Phelps*

SURREY

Cheam and Belmont, *P Berry*
Croydon, *S Bligh*
Dorking and District, *K Harding*
Around Dorking, *A Jackson*
Around Epsom, *P Berry*
Farnham: A Second Selection, *J Parratt*
Around Haslemere and Hindhead, *T Winter & G Collyer*
Richmond, *Richmond Local History Society*
Sutton, *P Berry*

SUSSEX

Arundel and the Arun Valley, *J Godfrey*
Bishopstone and Seaford, *P Pople & P Berry*
Brighton and Hove, *J Middleton*
Brighton and Hove: A Second Selection, *J Middleton*
Around Crawley, *M Goldsmith*
Hastings, *P Haines*
Hastings: A Second Selection, *P Haines*
Around Haywards Heath, *J Middleton*
Around Heathfield, *A Gillet & B Russell*
Around Heathfield: A Second Selection,
A Gillet & B Russell
High Weald, *B Harwood*
High Weald: A Second Selection, *B Harwood*
Horsham and District, *T Wales*
Lewes, *J Middleton*
RAF Tangmere, *A Saunders*
Around Rye, *A Dickinson*
Around Worthing, *S White*

WARWICKSHIRE

Along the Avon from Stratford to Tewkesbury, *J Jeremiah*
Bedworth, *J Burton*
Coventry, *D McGrory*
Around Coventry, *D McGrory*
Nuneaton, *S Cleus & S Vaughan*
Around Royal Leamington Spa, *J Cameron*
Around Royal Leamington Spa: A Second Selection,
J Cameron
Around Warwick, *R Booth*

WESTMORLAND

Eden Valley, *J Marsh*
Kendal, *M & P Duff*
South Westmorland Villages, *J Marsh*
Westmorland Lakes, *J Marsh*

WILTSHIRE

Around Amesbury, *P Daniels*
Chippenham and Lacock, *A Wilson & M Wilson*
Around Corsham and Box, *A Wilson & M Wilson*
Around Devizes, *D Buxton*
Around Highworth, *G Tanner*
Around Highworth and Faringdon, *G Tanner*
Around Malmesbury, *A Wilson*
Marlborough: A Second Selection, *P Colman*
Around Melksham,
Melksham and District Historical Association
Nadder Valley, *R. Sawyer*
Salisbury, *P Saunders*
Salisbury: A Second Selection, *P Daniels*
Salisbury: A Third Selection, *P Daniels*
Around Salisbury, *P Daniels*
Swindon: A Third Selection, *The Swindon Society*
Swindon: A Fourth Selection, *The Swindon Society*
Trowbridge, *M Marshman*
Around Wilton, *P Daniels*
Around Wootton Bassett, Cricklade and Purton, *T Sharp*

WORCESTERSHIRE

Evesham to Bredon, *F Archer*
Around Malvern, *K Smith*
Around Pershore, *M Dowty*
Redditch and the Needle District, *R Saunders*
Redditch: A Second Selection, *R Saunders*
Around Tenbury Wells, *D Green*
Worcester, *M Dowty*
Around Worcester, *R Jones*
Worcester in a Day, *M Dowty*
Worcestershire at Work, *R Jones*

YORKSHIRE

Huddersfield: A Second Selection, *H Wheeler*
Huddersfield: A Third Selection, *H Wheeler*
Leeds Road and Rail, *R Vickers*
Pontefract, *R van Riel*
Scarborough, *D Coggins*
Scarborough's War Years, *R Percy*
Skipton and the Dales, *Friends of the Craven Museum*
Around Skipton-in-Craven, *Friends of the Craven Museum*
Yorkshire Wolds, *I & M Sumner*